MW01119872

Exploring Our Rainforest

Spider Monkey

Susan H. Gray

Published in the United States of America by Cherry Lake Publishing
Ann Arbor, Michigan
www.cherrylakepublishing.com

Content Adviser: John Mitani, Primate Behavioral Ecologist, University of Michigan and Ngogo Chimpanzee Project
Reading Adviser: Marla Conn, ReadAbility, Inc.

Photo Credits: ©ChameleonsEye/Shutterstock Images, cover, 1, 26; ©Anup Shah/Thinkstock, 5; ©IUCN (International Union for Conservation of Nature) 2008, 6; ©Michael Fitzsimmons/Thinkstock, 7; ©Christian Vinces /Shutterstock Images, 9; ©Dorling Kindersley/Thinkstock, 10; ©outlook/iStock, 12; ©Wollertz/Shutterstock Images, 15; ©Anton_Ivanov/Shutterstock Images, 16; ©Kerstiny/Dreamstime.com, 19; ©holbox/Shutterstock Images, 20; ©Lukas Blazek/Dreamstime.com, 21; ©Casarsa/iStock, 23; ©DC_Colombia/iStock, 25; ©Mikelane45/Dreamstime.com, 27; ©Erni/Shutterstock Images, 29

Library of Congress Cataloging-in-Publication Data

Gray, Susan Heinrichs, author.
Spider monkey / Susan H. Gray.
pages cm. — (Exploring our rainforests)
Summary: "Introduces facts about spider monkeys, including physical features, habitat, life cycle, food, and threats to these rainforest creatures. Photos, captions, and keywords supplement the narrative of this informational text."
— Provided by publisher.
Audience: Ages 8-12.
Audience: Grades 4 to 6.
ISBN 978-1-63188-980-6 (hardcover) — ISBN 978-1-63362-019-3 (pbk.) —
ISBN 978-1-63362-058-2 (pdf) — ISBN 978-1-63362-097-1 (ebook) 1. Spider monkeys—Juvenile literature. I. Title.

QL737.P915G73 2014
599.8'58—dc23 2014020998

Cherry Lake Publishing would like to acknowledge the work of
The Partnership for 21st Century Skills. Please visit *www.p21.org*
for more information.

Printed in the United States of America
Corporate Graphics

ABOUT THE AUTHOR

Susan H. Gray has a master's degree in zoology. She has worked in research and has taught college-level science classes. Susan has also written more than 140 science and reference books, but especially likes to write about animals. She and her husband, Michael, live in Cabot, Arkansas.

TABLE OF CONTENTS

CHAPTER 1
CRAZY MONKEY! 4

CHAPTER 2
THE SPIDER MONKEY'S BODY 8

CHAPTER 3
MONKEY CHOW 14

CHAPTER 4
THE LIFE OF A SPIDER MONKEY .. 18

CHAPTER 5
TROUBLE IN THE TREETOPS 24

THINK ABOUT IT 30
LEARN MORE 31
GLOSSARY 32
INDEX 32

— CHAPTER 1 —

Crazy Monkey!

It's a warm evening, and the spider monkey is taking it easy. Resting high in a tree, he is just finishing a piece of fruit. He lazily turns his gaze downward. Suddenly, his eyes open wide. He sits up straight and begins screaming.

Far below him is a mother jaguar with her two cubs. They are padding slowly along the forest floor, hunting for a meal. But the jaguars stop in their tracks when the screaming begins. All three look up to see who is making such a fuss.

Spider monkeys scream when they feel threatened.

This agitates the monkey even more. He leaps to his feet. He shakes his head back and forth. He jumps up and down. He grabs a tree branch and shakes it hard. Finally, he breaks the branch off and flings it to the ground.

The branch lands nowhere near the jaguars. But it doesn't matter. All three trot deeper into the forest. They want nothing to do with this crazy monkey.

Spider monkeys are found in Mexico and in Central and South America. They live in tropical rainforests where it is warm and damp. They spend their days in the

The black-faced black spider monkey lives in the northern part of South America.

forest **canopy**, high above the ground. The canopy is dense with branches and leaves, and offers plenty of places for spider monkeys to explore, find food, sleep, and just hang out.

Spider monkeys also inhabit other types of forests. They live in wooded areas along rivers, in marshes, and on mountainsides. They especially prefer older forests with very tall trees.

Spider monkeys' fur can vary in color.

— CHAPTER 2 —

The Spider Monkey's Body

There are seven different spider monkey **species**. They all look basically the same. The monkeys are covered in fur and have long, spindly arms and legs. They also have remarkably long **prehensile** tails. The monkeys often hang by their tails and reach out to pick fruit. When hanging this way, with their skinny limbs moving around, they remind people of spiders. This is how they got their name.

The black spider monkey is the largest species. An adult male stands almost 2 feet (0.6 meters) tall. He weighs nearly 24 pounds (10.9 kg), about the same as a 2-year-old child.

Except for a few hairless areas of their bodies, these monkeys are covered in fur. Black-handed monkeys may have tan, brown, black, or reddish fur. Black spider monkeys are covered in long, glossy black fur. Some monkeys have light-colored or white bellies. And some have limbs and tails that are darker than the rest of their bodies.

Spider monkeys have very long arms and legs—and a long tail.

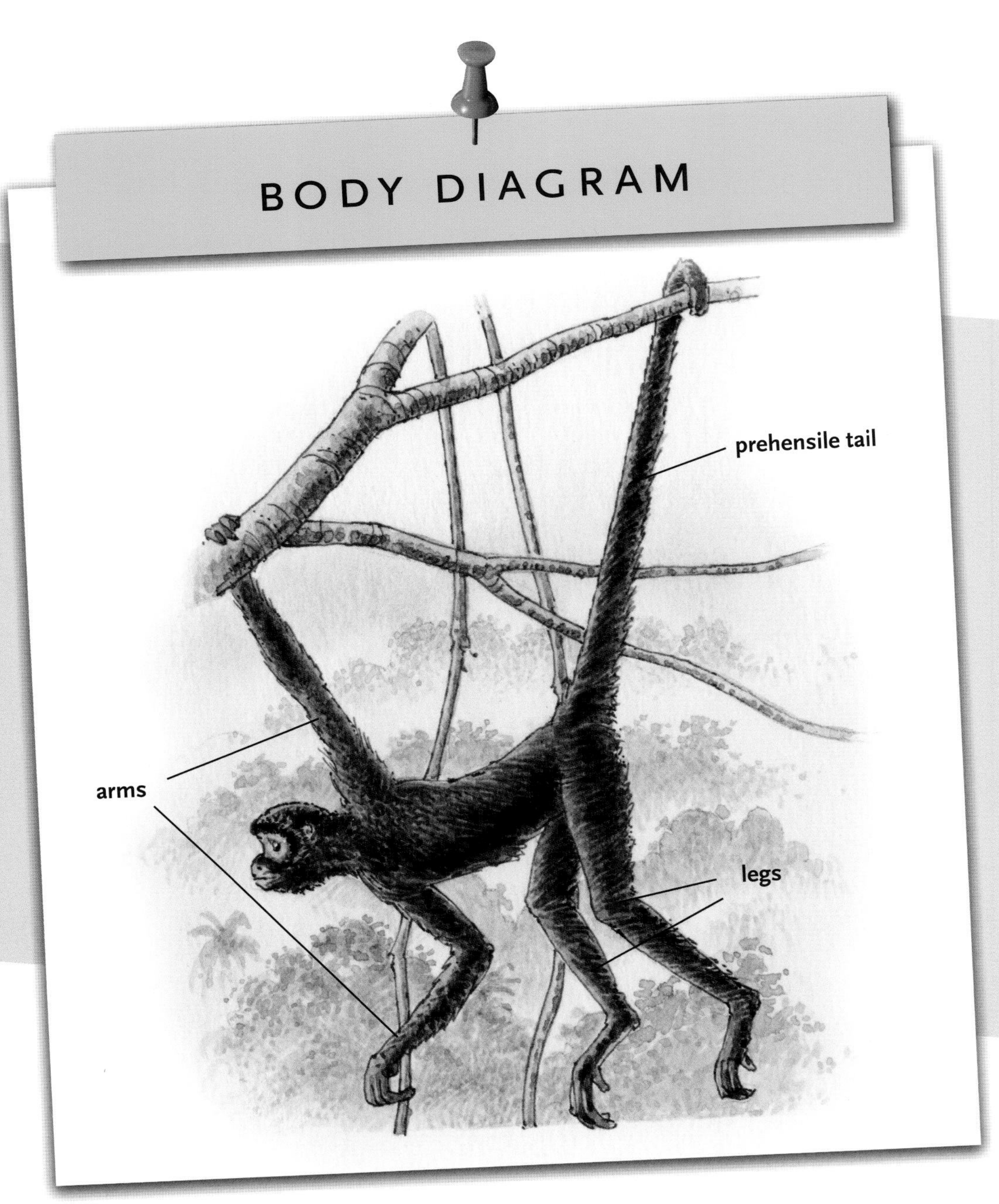

The monkey's tail helps it swing from tree to tree.

The monkeys have little or no fur around their lips, noses, and eyes. On the underside of the tail, each monkey has a bald patch. The skin of this patch is rough and has ridges. Such skin helps the monkey's tail cling to a tree branch without slipping.

Spider monkey arms and legs are quite long. These monkeys are real acrobats. They often travel by swinging, hand-over-hand, from branch to branch. This is called **brachiation**. When spider monkeys travel this way, they can get through the forest very quickly.

They also make flying leaps from tree to tree. Upon landing, they grab any branches available with their hands, feet, and tail.

The hands of the spider monkey are long and slender. The fingers naturally curl inward into a hook shape. Thumbs either appear as little stubs or are completely absent.

The arm and hand bones are ideal for a brachiating animal. The wrists are especially flexible. The hooklike

Powerful muscles in a spider monkey's tail allow it hang from a tree branch.

hands latch easily onto branches. The monkeys' elbow joints can withstand the stress of swinging and hanging.

Their legs and feet are also long and slim. The big toe on each foot sticks out and can be used like a thumb. When walking along branches, that toe helps the monkey to grab and hold on tight.

Incredibly, the spider monkey's tail is longer than the rest of its body. It contains about 25 bones and has extremely powerful muscles. When hanging by the tail, the monkey is able to pull itself almost to a horizontal position. At the end of the tail, the more powerful muscles are on the underside. These muscles allow the monkey to curl its tail inward and strongly grip a tree branch.

The tail can do more than grab branches. When the monkey walks along a branch or on the forest floor, its tail helps keep the animal balanced. It's also so flexible that it can actually pick up nuts.

The monkey's brain and nerves control the activities of the tail. In fact, the brain center that controls tail movement is unusually large. You might say that the spider monkey's tail has a mind of its own.

THINK ABOUT IT

WHAT IF THE SPIDER MONKEY HAD THUMBS? DO YOU THINK THAT WOULD HELP THE MONKEY GRAB ON TO BRANCHES ANY BETTER? WHY OR WHY NOT?

CHAPTER 3

Monkey Chow

Spider monkeys eat all sorts of things, but their main food is fruit. When ripe fruit is plentiful, they eat little else. They can dangle by their tails from one branch and use their long arms to reach fruit on other branches. But what if fruit becomes difficult to find? They will feed on leaves, flowers, nuts, bird eggs, insects, and even the bark of trees.

These monkeys don't need to drink much water. Instead, they get most of their water from the fruit they eat. Fruit is also a high-sugar, high-energy food. This is exactly the right food for active, tree-swinging monkeys.

Fruit is a large part of the spider monkey's diet.

Spider monkeys climb high into the trees to pick the fruit that grows there.

Many of these fruits are loaded with seeds. The monkeys swallow the seeds whole. They are not digested but wind up in the monkeys' droppings. As they travel, the monkeys spread their seed-filled droppings throughout the forest. In time, new little trees sprout from the seeds. This helps the forest to survive.

The spider monkey's teeth are perfect for its fruity diet. The teeth in front are long and wide. Animals use these front teeth for cutting into food. Fruit-eating spider monkeys need such teeth for cutting through peels and rinds. The monkeys' cheek teeth are small, though. These teeth are used for chewing and grinding. Monkeys don't need to chew their soft, juicy fruit very much, so their small grinding teeth work just fine.

GO DEEPER

SCIENTISTS HAVE STUDIED WHICH FOODS SPIDER MONKEYS PREFER OVER OTHERS. BESIDES THE TASTE, WHY MIGHT A MONKEY PREFER A CERTAIN FOOD?

— CHAPTER 4 —

THE LIFE OF A SPIDER MONKEY

Spider monkey mothers have only one baby at a time. The baby has thin wispy fur, large eyes, and long, skinny arms and legs. During its first few months, the baby clings to its mother's chest and belly. The mother provides milk for and protects her infant, often wrapping her arms around it.

After about 5 or 6 months, the young monkey is able to ride around on its mother's back. From this position, it gets a better view of the world. Soon, it's off exploring on its own or playing with other young monkeys. Such adventures are always brief, though. The young monkey never strays far from its mom. Even after its first year, it still stays close to her and occasionally rides on her back.

The baby spider monkey depends on its mother for traveling around.

In time, the young monkey learns to brachiate. It even attempts little leaps between branches. The mother is never far away when her young one is learning these skills.

Sometimes, a mother does a remarkable thing. When she sees a big gap between branches, she knows her youngster can't leap such a distance. So she forms a bridge with her body. Using her hands, feet, and tail, she grasps branches and hangs on tight, holding steady while her little one crawls across.

As the monkey grows up, it gets to know the other monkeys in its group. Spider monkeys usually live in troops of 20 to 30 individuals who share the same

The spider monkey mother must teach her baby how to swing from tree to tree.

territory. These troops split up into smaller groups, called parties, that spread out to find food. When the small groups come back together, all the monkeys greet one another. They call out, play, entwine their tails, sniff, and hug one another.

Spider monkeys are social animals who like to play with one another.

Group life provides safety for the monkeys. If one spider monkey spots a **predator** nearby, he immediately becomes disturbed. He shakes his head, barks or screams, rattles tree branches, and throws things. Such behavior can drive the predator away. It also alerts other monkeys to the danger.

In general, spider monkeys take around 5 years to become adults. Then they are ready to mate and have babies of their own. Spider monkeys often live into their 20s and 30s.

This young spider monkey still has a lot to learn about life in the rainforest.

LOOK AGAIN

LOOK AT THE PHOTO OF THE BABY SPIDER MONKEY. HOW DOES THE YOUNG MONKEY ALREADY LOOK LIKE ITS PARENTS?

TROUBLE IN THE TREETOPS

Spider monkeys become pretty upset when they see predators. But how can these monkeys have any enemies? Why aren't they safe living so high up in the trees?

Part of the problem is that the monkeys *are* so high in the trees. There, they have to deal with one of the forest's most powerful predators—the harpy eagle. These birds spend most of their time in the rainforest canopy. They excel at flying through dense, leafy areas. A harpy can easily snatch a small monkey from its perch.

Harpy eagles often target spider monkeys when hunting.

When spider monkeys leave the trees for the forest floor, they need to be wary of predators.

Spider monkeys spend little time on the forest floor—they're not safe there, either. Meat-eating jaguars prowl the rainforest. Large, hungry snakes also pose a danger.

Younger monkeys are always at a disadvantage. They can't escape danger as quickly as their parents. They can't run or brachiate as well as adult monkeys. They can't make great leaps between trees. But young spider monkeys stay close to their mothers for many months. Hitching a ride with mom is a good way to flee from danger.

Predators are not the spider monkeys' only problem.

In some places, people hunt them for food. Their large size makes them attractive game. And because they make such a loud racket when alarmed, they are easy to find.

Another problem is the destruction of forest land. People cut trees for lumber and clear land to plant crops. This means the loss of the spider monkey's **habitat**. Monkeys need lots of room to do well. They also need an abundant food supply.

Without enough trees, spider monkeys would have nowhere to live.

The International Union for the Conservation of Nature (IUCN) says almost all the spider monkey species are **endangered**, but some are in more trouble than others. Because the rainforests are being cut down so quickly, someday the monkeys might completely disappear.

Even if hunting and forest destruction stopped, that would not solve all the spider monkeys' problems. Spider monkey mothers give birth to only one baby at a time. And their babies are spaced several years apart. As a result, the monkey population increases very slowly. It would take many years for an endangered species to recover.

Spider monkeys, the acrobats of the rainforest, are amazing little animals. They are smart and know how to scare intruders away. We hope spider monkeys will be with us for many years to come.

Because its arms and legs are so long, people say this monkey looks like a spider.

LOOK AGAIN

LOOK CLOSELY AT THIS PICTURE OF A SPIDER MONKEY. WHAT ARE YOU ABLE TO LEARN FROM THIS PHOTO THAT YOU HAVEN'T LEARNED FROM READING THIS BOOK?

THINK ABOUT IT

- Chapter 1 mentions a family of jaguars. Which poses the greater danger to the spider monkey—the two cubs or the single adult?
- Chapter 2 discusses the monkey's prehensile tail. Can you think of another animal with a prehensile tail? How does that animal use its tail?
- What was the most interesting piece of information you learned about spider monkeys?
- Some people buy spider monkeys to keep as pets. Why is this a bad idea?
- Chapter 5 discusses habitat loss. What are some ways to help stop the destruction of the forests?

LEARN MORE

FURTHER READING

Aloian, Molly, and Bobbie Kalman. *Endangered Monkeys.* New York: Crabtree Publishing Company, 2007.

Franchino, Vicky. *Spider Monkeys.* Danbury, CT: Children's Press, 2014.

Redmond, Ian. *Gorilla, Monkey & Ape.* New York: DK Children, 2000.

WEB SITES

Learning About Rainforests—Spider Monkey
www.srl.caltech.edu/personnel/krubal/rainforest/Edit560s6/www/animals/spidermonkeypage.html
Read about spider monkeys and find links to pages about other rainforest animals.

Los Angeles Zoo & Botanical Gardens—Mammals
www.lazoo.org/animals/mammals/
Read descriptions of many animals, including the black-handed spider monkey and the jaguar.

Philadelphia Zoo—Colombian Black Spider Monkey
www.philadelphiazoo.org/Animals/Mammals/Primates/Columbian-Black-Spider-Monkey.aspx
Find brief information on one of the spider monkey species, along with links to similar pages on other primates.

GLOSSARY

brachiation (bray-kee-AY-shuhn) traveling by swinging by the arms from one hold to the next

canopy (KAN-uh-pee) the cover formed by the leafy upper tree branches in a forest

endangered (en-DAYN-jerd) at risk of dying out

habitat (HAB-ih-tat) the place where a plant or animal naturally lives

predator (PRED-uh-tur) an animal that hunts and eats other animals

prehensile (pree-HEN-suhl) able to grasp something

species (SPEE-sheez) particular kinds or types of living things

INDEX

babies, 18–20, 28
body, 8–13
brachiation, 11, 20

canopy, 6

food, 14–17
fur, 7, 8, 9, 11

habitat, 5–7, 27
humans, 27–28

life cycle, 18–22

predators, 22, 24–26

screaming, 4–5
seeds, 17
size, 8

tail, 8, 9, 10, 11, 12–13
teeth, 17
threats, 5, 27–28
troops, 20–22